HARDWOOD GREATS
PRO BASKETBALL'S BEST PLAYERS

KEVIN DURANT

HARDWOOD GREATS

PRO BASKETBALL'S BEST PLAYERS

CHRIS PAUL

GIANNIS ANTETOKOUNMPO

JAMES HARDEN

KEVIN DURANT

LEBRON JAMES

PAUL GEORGE

RUSSELL WESTBROOK

STEPHEN CURRY

HARDWOOD GREATS

PRO BASKETBALL'S BEST PLAYERS

KEVIN DURANT

DONALD PARKER

MASON CREST

PHILADELPHIA

MIAMI

Mason Crest
450 Parkway Drive, Suite D
Broomall, Pennsylvania 19008
(866) MCP-BOOK (toll-free)
www.masoncrest.com

First printing
9 8 7 6 5 4 3 2 1

ISBN (hardback) 978-1-4222-4348-0
ISBN (series) 978-1-4222- 4344-2
ISBN (ebook) 978-1-4222- 7463-7

Cataloging-in-Publication Data on file with the Library of Congress

Developed and Produced by National Highlights Inc.
Editor: Andrew Luke
Interior and cover design: Annalisa Gumbrecht, Studio Gumbrecht
Production: Michelle Luke

QR CODES AND LINKS TO THIRD-PARTY CONTENT

CONTENTS

KEY ICONS TO LOOK FOR:

Words to Understand: These words with their easy-to-understand definitions will increase the reader's understanding of the text while building vocabulary skills.

Sidebars: This boxed material within the main text allows readers to build knowledge, gain insights, explore possibilities, and broaden their perspectives by weaving together additional information to provide realistic and holistic perspectives.

Educational Videos: Readers can view videos by scanning our QR codes, providing them with additional educational content to supplement the text. Examples include news coverage, moments in history, speeches, iconic sports moments, and much more!

Text-Dependent Questions: These questions send the reader back to the text for more careful attention to the evidence presented there.

Research Projects: Readers are pointed toward areas of further inquiry connected to each chapter. Suggestions are provided for projects that encourage deeper research and analysis.

Series Glossary of Key Terms: This back-of-the-book glossary contains terminology used throughout this series. Words found here increase the reader's ability to read and comprehend higher-level books and articles in this field.

WORDS TO UNDERSTAND

boon: A timely benefit

milestone: A significant point in development

wunderkind: One who succeeds in a competitive or highly difficult field or profession at an early age

CHAPTER 1

GREATEST MOMENTS

DURANT'S NBA CAREER

It didn't take long for Kevin Durant to establish himself as one of the greats in the game today. Drafted with the second pick overall by the then Seattle Supersonics (now, the Oklahoma City Thunder) in the 2007 NBA draft, he has risen to claim a place among the very best players, such as LeBron James, Dwyane Wade, Stephen Curry, and James Harden.

Durant has won two NBA (National Basketball Association) championships, been named Rookie of the Year and Player of the Year, and has seen action in nine straight All-Star games. He joined the 20,000-points-scored club in the 2017–2018 season. Durant has played alongside several other great players including former Oklahoma City teammates Russell Westbrook and James Harden, as well as Stephen Curry as a member of the Golden State Warriors. In 2019, he chose to play in Brooklyn alongside Kyrie Irving.

Looking at the most talked about (and best) players in the NBA today, Durant ranks highly among his peers in nearly every important statistical category (through their first five full seasons in the league):

PLAYER	TEAM	G	PTS	TRB	AST	FG%	3P%	FT%	PPG
LeBron James*	CLE	391	10,689	2,694	2,572	46.7%	32.4%	72.8%	27.3
Kevin Durant*	SEA/OKC	380	9,978	2,513	1,073	46.8%	36.4%	87.8%	26.3
Russell Westbrook*	OKC	394	7,832	1,908	2,726	43.2%	30.2%	81.4%	19.9
Stephen Curry*	GSW	336	6,814	1,378	2,247	46.7%	44.0%	89.6%	20.3
Giannis Antetokounmpo*	MIL	393	6,751	2,946	1,497	50.6%	28.4%	74.6%	17.2
James Harden*	OKC/HOU	371	6,669	1,474	1,443	44.5%	36.9%	84.9%	18.0

Highlight indicates the leader for the statistical category
  * Named Most Valuable Player in the NBA

Durant joined forces with Stephen Curry at Golden State in 2016.

Here is a look at those same players' career season averages. As you can see, Durant ranks very high compared to the league's best players:

PLAYER	G	PTS	TRB	AST	FG%	3P%	FT%	PPG
LeBron James	75	2,034	555	541	50.4%	34.3%	73.6%	27.2
Kevin Durant	*71*	*1,911*	*499*	*291*	*49.2%*	*38.1%*	*88.3%*	*27.0*
James Harden	77	1,715	400	474	44.33%	36.5%	85.7%	24.3
Russell Westbrook	75	1,911	524	627	43.4%	30.8%	80.1%	23.0
Stephen Curry	69	1,632	313	459	47.7%	43.6%	90.5%	23.5
Giannis Antetokounmpo	78	1,458	641	320	52.1%	27.7%	74.2%	18.8

Highlight indicates the leader for the statistical category

There is no doubt that any conversation about who the best players are in the NBA must include Kevin Durant. He has sharpened his skills as a shooter and floor general, becoming one of the leading stars of the NBA. He looks to have several more great years ahead of him, and if he continues to play at the rate that he has been, he may well be regarded as one of the greatest players in NBA history!

DURANT'S GREATEST CAREER MOMENTS

HERE IS A LIST OF

SOME OF THE CAREER

FIRSTS AND GREATEST

ACHIEVEMENTS DURING

HIS TIME IN THE NBA:

Durant won the NBA MVP award following the 2013–2014 season with Oklahoma City. He led the league in scoring by averaging 32 points per game.

SCORED 10,000 POINTS IN HIS CAREER

Durant began the 2012–2013 NBA seasons with high hopes. Coming off a disappointing NBA Finals loss to LeBron James and the Miami Heat, he wanted to keep Oklahoma City headed in the right direction toward hopefully a repeat Western Conference championship and NBA Finals trophy. He entered the season having scored 9,978 points in his career. In a game against the San Antonio Spurs, the first game of the new season (November 1, 2012), he needed only 22 points to join the elite list of players with 10,000 or more points scored in a career. How did he do? He scored 23.

Durant entered the 2012–2013 NBA season needing 22 points to reach 10,000 points. He accomplished this with a point to spare in an opening-season game against San Antonio on November 1, 2012.

SCORED 20,000 POINTS IN HIS CAREER

As a member of the Golden State Warriors, Durant achieved yet another scoring **milestone** by reaching 20,000 points scored in a career. This occurred in a game on January 10, 2018, against the Los Angeles Clippers. Durant scored 40 points on 14-for-18 shooting in a 125–106 loss. The 40-point effort, however, added his name to the list of players who have scored at least 20,000 points. He jumped ahead of Kobe Bryant by nineteen days as the second-youngest player to accomplish this.

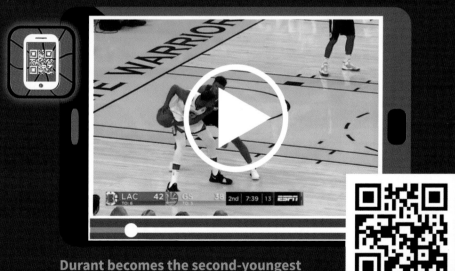

Durant becomes the second-youngest player at age twenty-nine (the youngest being LeBron James of the Los Angeles Lakers) to score 20,000 points for his career in a January 10, 2018, game against the Los Angeles Clippers.

NAMED NBA ROOKIE OF THE YEAR (FOR THE 2007-2008 SEASON)

Durant came out of the University of Texas as one of the most celebrated freshman in men's college basketball history. He was honored as Player of the Year, Big 12 Conference Player of the Year, and various other honors, helping him make the decision to leave early and make the jump from college to the NBA. Taken with the second pick, he turned in a phenomenal rookie season for the Seattle Supersonics. He averaged 20.3 points per game (scoring 1,624 points), 4.4 rebounds, and 2.4 assists per game. These totals were good enough for him to be named Rookie of the Year for the 2007–2008 season.

Song (from Rocky)

Durant did not miss a step transitioning from college to the pros. His rookie season in the NBA ended with his being named the league's top rookie in 2008. He became the first (and last) Sonics player to win Rookie of the Year honors.

NAMED MOST VALUABLE PLAYER OF THE 2016-2017 NBA FINALS

Durant left for Golden State before the 2016 season. He joined a Warriors squad that had just come off the best regular season performance in NBA history (73–9). The team came up short in the NBA Finals, losing to the Cleveland Cavaliers. The addition of Durant was a **boon** for the Warriors, who won 67 games in the regular season. They again faced the Cavaliers in the NBA Finals. The trio of Durant, Stephen Curry, and Klay Thompson beat the Cavs in five games. Durant's 35.2 points per game, 5.4 assists per game, and 6.8 rebounds per game in the finals earned him MVP honors.

Durant was the difference-maker for the Golden State Warriors after joining the squad for the 2016–2017 season. He helped the team avenge the previous year's NBA Finals loss against Cleveland, scoring 35.2 points per game to earn MVP honors.

NAMED NBA MOST VALUABLE PLAYER, 2013-2014

Durant was honored in college as the best player by winning the Naismith Award as a freshman at the University of Texas. He brought his talents as a **wunderkind** of the game to the NBA, and by his seventh season in the NBA he had worked his way up to the top (with the Oklahoma City Thunder). He led the NBA in field goals made and attempted (849/1,688), free throws made and attempted (703/805), points scored (2,593), and points-per-game average (32). These numbers not only helped Durant get named to the All-Star team and make first team All-NBA, it also helped him earn honors as the league's Most Valuable Player.

Durant's 2013–2014 season with the Thunder was one of the best of his career. He led the NBA in total points and was rewarded for his efforts with league MVP honors.

6

WON FIRST NBA SCORING TITLE, 2009-2010

Durant has led the league in scoring in four out of five consecutive seasons (2010–2012; 2014). This began in 2009–2010, where he scored 2,472 points as a member of the Thunder, for a per-game average of 30.1 points. Durant also led the league that season in free throws made. Hitting 47.6 percent of his field goals attempted and 90 percent of his free throws contributed to his taking the scoring title in his third professional season. The accomplishment was even more incredible when considering who the runners-up for the title were: LeBron James, second at 29.7 ppg, and Carmelo Anthony, third at 28.2 ppg.

DEN 71 OKC 70

Durant leads all NBA scorers in the 2009–2010 season with 30.1 ppg to win his first scoring title.

WON FIRST NBA CHAMPIONSHIP, 2016-2017

Durant led a star-studded Oklahoma City team featuring himself, Russell Westbrook, and James Harden to the 2012 NBA Finals. Despite a great effort by the trio, the Thunder came up short to the Miami Heat. After departing the Thunder for Golden State in 2017, Durant went to the NBA Finals with the Warriors and helped the team defeat Cleveland in five games (Durant was the leading scorer and MVP) to claim his first NBA title.

**After losing to the Miami Heat in the 2011–2012 NBA Finals as a member of the Oklahoma City Thunder, Durant retooled and joined the Golden State Warriors.
In his first season as a Warrior (2016–2017) he helped lead a 67-win, 15-loss team to the NBA Finals where they beat the Cleveland Cavaliers 4–1 for his first NBA championship.**

BACK-TO-BACK CHAMPIONSHIPS AND FINALS MVPS

To conclude the 2017–2018 NBA season, Durant and the Warriors once again faced Cleveland in the finals. Durant was dominant, as he had been the previous year, averaging 28.8 ppg, 10.8 rebounds per game, and 7.5 assists per game. This includes a career-high 43 points for Durant in Game 3 of what was a four-game sweep of the Cavaliers. To go along with his second consecutive championship, Durant earned a second finals MVP award as well.

Watch highlights of Durant scoring a career playoff-high 43 points in Game 3 of the 2018 NBA Finals.

With his two championship wins with the Warriors, Durant's career now stacks up to those of some of the best players to ever play in the NBA.

TEXT-DEPENDENT QUESTIONS

1. How many points did Durant average per game in the 2016–2017 NBA Finals?

2. Against which opponent did Durant score 10,000 NBA career points? What was the date of that game?

3. What year was Durant named the league's most valuable player? What team did he play for that season? What years did he win MVP honors in the NBA Finals?

 # RESEARCH PROJECT

Durant was named the Naismith Player of the Year while in college. He was the first freshman in NCAA history to be so honored. He also was named Rookie of the Year for the 2007–2008 NBA season and NBA Most Valuable Player for the 2013–2014 season. It is rare for a player to be honored as the best player in college, the best rookie, and the best player in the NBA. In fact, only five players (including Durant) have achieved all three honors in their careers so far. Do some research and determine who the other players were who were named the Naismith College Player of the Year, NBA Rookie of the Year, and NBA Most Valuable Player.

WORDS TO UNDERSTAND

eerie: Having or seeming to have a supernatural or inexplicable basis so as to inspire superstitious fear; weird

esteemed: Highly regarded and valued accordingly

tutelage: Instruction, especially of an individual

CHAPTER 2

THE ROAD TO THE TOP

KEVIN DURANT'S PERFORMANCE AS A PLAYER

Kevin Wayne Durant was born in Washington, DC, on September 29, 1988. His parents, Wanda Durant and Wayne Pratt, split up when he was a baby, eventually divorcing and leaving him to be raised by his mother and by his grandmother, Barbara Davis, in Suitland, Maryland, located ten miles (16 km) southeast of Washington, DC. Durant was raised alongside two brothers (Tony and Rayvonne) and a sister (Brianna).

Durant began competing in basketball through a relationship he developed with a local Amateur Athletic Union (AAU) coach named Taras Brown (who became a father figure for Durant), at the Seat Pleasant (Maryland) Activity Center. By age thirteen, his father (who works as a police officer on the U.S.

Capitol Police force at the Library of Congress in DC) became a part of his life again and traveled with him across the country to various basketball tournaments.

Durant was unusually tall for his age by the time he reached middle school. He reached the height of six feet (1.83 m) at age thirteen. He used the height advantage he had over other players at that age to work on the essential skills he would need to compete at the next level. This development, under the **tutelage** of Brown and assistant coach Charles Craig, resulted in Durant making the McDonald's All-American team. He grew to 6 feet 8 inches (2.03 m) by his sophomore year in high school. This made him an imposing figure on the court and in position to chart his path to the NBA.

Durant's father, Wayne Pratt, works for the U.S. Capitol Police at the Library of Congress. He came back into Durant's life when Durant was thirteen.

HIGH SCHOOL

Durant began high school playing for National Christian Academy (nickname: Eagles), located in neighboring Fort Washington, Maryland (adjacent to Washington, DC). He spent the first two years of his high school time playing for the Eagles. It took him awhile to get into the flow of play as he had a difficult time getting along with older players. Although he was their size physically, the older players often denied him the ball, and some refused to play with the younger underclassman.

Durant thought about quitting basketball as a freshman. His mother convinced him to continue to work hard and "earn the respect" of the older players if he wanted to succeed. That advice, coupled with the growth spurt he experienced between his freshman and sophomore years, helped Durant earn respect and assert himself as a leader on the team.

 ## THE MEANING OF NUMBER 35

Durant signed a letter of intent to play at the University of Texas in Austin, Texas, in 2006. The highlight of the signing was for him to have his favorite AAU coach, Charles Craig, at his side while he performed the task. Unfortunately, the coach was the victim of a senseless crime, which cost him his life at age thirty-five. Durant was so close to the coach that he sought to memorialize him by wearing Craig's age at the time of his murder on his jersey. He did so for 12 NBA seasons before switching to number 7 after his move to the Nets in 2019.

NBA DRAFT DAY 2007 SIGNIFICANT ACCOUNTS

- Kevin Durant was selected by Seattle (now Oklahoma City) with the second pick in the first round of the 2007 NBA draft.

- The 2007 NBA draft was held at New York City's Madison Square Garden on June 28, 2007.

- Durant was the first forward drafted in the 2007 NBA draft.

- He was one of twenty-eight forwards taken in the 2007 NBA draft (out of the sixty players drafted in rounds 1 and 2).

- The Portland Trailblazers had the most draft selections in 2007 with five, including the number-one overall pick (Greg Oden, Ohio State University). Four teams had one pick each in the draft: Memphis Grizzlies, New York Knicks, Orlando Magic, and Sacramento Kings. Four teams did not have a selection in the 2007 draft: Cleveland

Cavaliers, Denver Nuggets, Indiana Pacers, and Toronto Raptors.

- Oden and Durant were the first college freshmen ever to be taken with the top two picks in the NBA draft.

- Of the sixty players drafted in 2012, nine were drafted out of the Southeastern Conference (SEC), seven players came from the Atlantic Coast Conference (ACC), and six from the Big Ten Conference, representing nearly one-third of all of the players drafted.

- Eleven foreign-born players were selected in the 2007 draft, the most at the time (since surpassed by the 2012 and 2016 NBA drafts).

- Five players (including four starters) from the University of Florida (nickname: Gators), winners of the 2006–2007 NCAA Men's Basketball Championship, were drafted in the 2007 NBA draft: Al Horford, Atlanta Hawks (third pick overall), Corey Brewer, Minnesota Timberwolves (seventh pick overall), Joakim Noah, Chicago Bulls (ninth pick overall), Chris Richard, Minnesota Timberwolves (forty-first pick), and Taurean Green, Portland Trailblazers (fifty-second pick). Three players for the runner-up Ohio State University (nickname: Buckeyes) men's basketball team were drafted, including number-one overall pick Greg Oden (Portland Trailblazers), Mike Conley, Memphis Grizzlies (fourth pick overall), and Daequan Cook, Philadelphia 76ers (twenty-first pick).

- For the first time in NBA draft history, three players from the same school (Florida) were picked in the top ten.

Source: https://stats.nba.com/draft/history/?Season=2007—NBA draft information for 2007 NBA draft.

Durant played his junior year of high school at Oak Hill Academy in Virginia, a school that has produced more than thirty NBA players, including ten-time All-Star Carmelo Anthony.

Durant honors his former AAU coach who through a tragic event died at that same age as the number 35 he wore on his jersey for most of his career.

He transferred to the famous Oak Hill Academy (nickname: Warriors) in Mouth of Wilson, Virginia (located 352 miles, or 567 km, southwest of DC), for his junior year, and finally to Montrose Christian School (nickname: Lions) in Rockville, Maryland. The school, a nationally ranked powerhouse in high school basketball, eliminated the boys' basketball program in 2015 and has since closed its doors.

HIGH SCHOOL SPECIAL EVENTS

Durant was invited to play in three **esteemed** high school all-star games in his senior year. They were:

- McDonald's All-American, March 29, 2006 (San Diego, CA)

- Nike Hoop Summit, April 8, 2006 (Memphis, TN)

- Jordan Brand Classic, April 22, 2006 (New York, NY)

EVENT	FG	FG%	3P	3P%	FT	FT%	TRB	AST	STL	BLK	PTS
McDonald's All-American	10	58.8%	2	33.3%	3	100.0%	5	4	2	0	25
Nike Hoop Summit	7	46.7%	2	40.0%	4	100.0%	7	1	0	1	20
Jordan Brand Classic	5	35.7%	2	40.0%	4	100.0%	7	4	0	3	16

Durant played alongside the top players in the country, including Greg Oden and Mike Conley, both of whom played together at Ohio State University and were also members of the 2007 NBA draft class. How was his performance in these three games? At the McDonald's All-American game, Durant earned MVP honors as his West team won 112–94. He led all scorers in the game with 25 points scored.

The following week Durant played for the U.S. team that beat the World squad 109–91. He scored 20 points with seven rebounds and 46.7 percent

Durant played in the 2006 edition of the annual McDonald's All-American game.

POSS

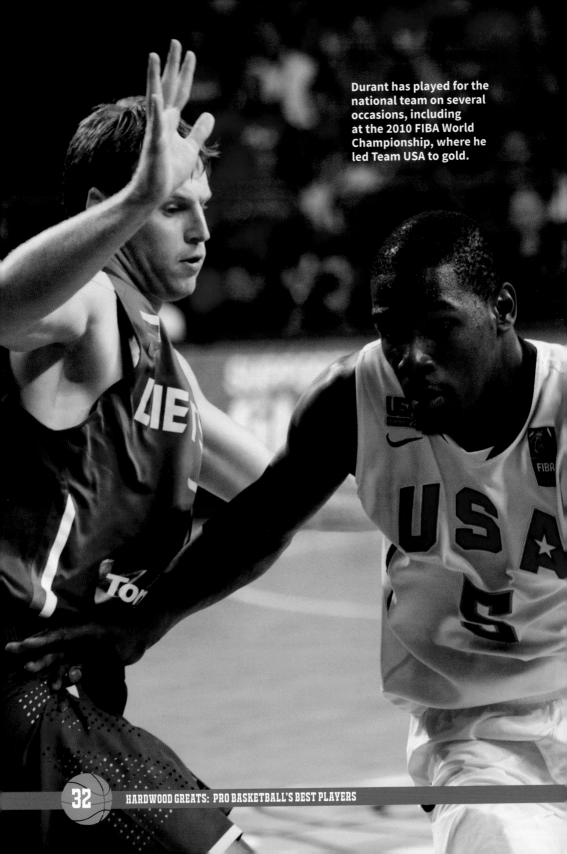

Durant has played for the national team on several occasions, including at the 2010 FIBA World Championship, where he led Team USA to gold.

shooting. He appeared before 9,400 spectators at New York's Madison Square Garden in the Jordan Brand Classic where he was co-MVP.

In 2007, Durant was ranked as the second-best player overall in the country, behind Greg Oden of Lawrence North High School in Indianapolis, Indiana. Oden was named the 2005 and 2006 National High School Player of the Year by several sources including Gatorade, McDonald's, Naismith, *Parade*, and *USA Today*.

Several schools sought Durant, including Louisville University, University of Kentucky, Georgia Tech University, University of Connecticut, and University of Texas. Oddly, one of the schools from his home state that did not seriously recruit him was the University of Maryland at College Park, which is 20.9 miles (32.2 km) north of his home in Suitland, Maryland. He chose to attend the University of Texas.

COLLEGE

Durant entered Texas as a freshman in the fall of 2006 and had an immediate impact on coach Rick Barnes' team. He had now grown to his present height of six feet nine inches (2.1 m). Durant led the team with a 25.8 points-per-game average and helped the Longhorns to a 25–10 overall record. He led the Big 12 Conference in scoring, rebounding, blocked shots, and defensive rebounds.

Texas received a number-four seed in the 2007 NCAA Men's Basketball tournament. Despite a 30-point scoring effort in a second-round match-up against the University of Southern California (USC), the team was ousted from the tournament. These are Durant's statistics for the only season that he played at the University of Texas:

G	FG	FGA	FG%	3P	3PA	3P%	FT	FTA	FT%	TRB	AST	STL	BLK	PTS
35	306	647	47.3%	82	203	40.4%	209	256	81.6%	390	46	66	67	903
35	306	647	47.3%	82	203	40.4%	209	256	81.6%	390	46	66	67	903

Durant left Texas after his freshman year and entered the 2007 NBA draft. He was named a consensus first team All-American and Big 12 Conference Player of the Year. He won the Dr. James Naismith College Player of the Year Award for the 2006–2007 season as well as the following awards:

- John R. Wooden Award for Most Outstanding Men's College Basketball Players
- Adolph F. Rupp Trophy for top player in men's Division I NCAA basketball
- AP Player of the Year
- NABC Player of the Year
- USBWA Oscar Robertson Trophy
- CBS/Chevrolet Player of the Year
- *Sporting News* Player of the Year
- USBWA Freshman of the Year
- *Sporting News* Freshman of the Year

Although he played only a single season at the University of Texas, the Longhorns retired Durant's number in 2009.

2007 first overall NBA draft pick Greg Oden dunks the ball in one of only 82 career games he played for Portland in five seasons. Injuries limited his NBA career to a total of 105 games in seven years.

Durant is the first freshman in the history of NCAA men's basketball to be named player of the year.

THE TALE OF TWO DRAFTS: GREG ODEN VS. KEVIN DURANT—SAM BOWIE VS. MICHAEL JORDAN

The 2007 draft that saw Greg Oden of Ohio State University drafted number-one overall by the Portland Trailblazers, and Durant selected with the number-two pick by the Seattle Supersonics was **eerily** similar to the one that took place in 1984. Michael Jordan, arguably the greatest player in NBA history, was drafted with the number-three pick in the 1984 NBA draft out of the University of North Carolina by the Chicago Bulls. He was picked behind University of Kentucky center Sam Bowie, who was selected by the Portland Trailblazers, the same team that drafted Oden.

Portland would come to regret their selection of Oden as they did nearly twenty years prior with the selection of Bowie. Both men never lived up to the expectations placed on them for being such high draft selections. Injuries affected both of their careers, and it has left many to wonder what would have become of the Trailblazers had they drafted Jordan in 1984 over Bowie and Durant in 2007 instead of Oden.

Bowie versus Jordan (Selections two and three, 1984 NBA draft)

PLAYER	TEAM	G/GS	FG	FGA	FT	FTA	TRB	AST	STL	BLK	PTS
Sam Bowie	POR	76/62	299	557	160	225	656	215	55	203	758
Michael Jordan	CHI	82/82	837	1,625	630	746	534	481	196	69	2,313

Oden versus Durant (Selections one and two, 2007 NBA draft)

PLAYER	TEAM	G/GS	FG	FGA	FT	FTA	TRB	AST	STL	BLK	PTS
Greg Oden*	POR	61/39	198	351	144	226	424	31	25	69	540
Kevin Durant	SEA	74/74	661	1,390	452	524	482	205	96	53	1,871

*Stats are from the 2008 NBA season, the first full season both Oden and
 Durant played (due to an injury that kept Oden out of the 2007 season).

TEXT-DEPENDENT QUESTIONS

1. How many brothers does Durant have? Where did he grow up?

2. How many high schools did Durant attend? What is the name of the school he attended as a senior in high school?

3. How many seasons did Durant play at the University of Texas?

RESEARCH PROJECT

Durant played alongside several current NBA players while in high school. One player was Michael Beasley of the Los Angeles Lakers. Beasley attended National Christian Academy with him (Beasley grew up in nearby Cheverly, Maryland, and the two remain friends to this day) and was also a McDonald's All-Star Game MVP and Consensus All-American while playing at Kansas State University (nickname: Wildcats)—both of which happened a year after Durant accomplished the same. Find three other players that attended one of the three high schools Durant went to and who became All-Americans in college and were selected in the first round of the NBA draft.

WORDS TO UNDERSTAND

garner: Causing fear, apprehension, or dread

inaugural: Marking the beginning of a new venture, series, season, etc.

tenure: The period or term of holding something

CHAPTER 3

ON THE COURT

DURANT'S NBA ACCOMPLISHMENTS

Durant brought his talents and skills to Seattle after being selected with the number-two overall pick in the 2007 NBA draft. Although the team finished with a 20–62 record that season and a fifth-place finish in the Pacific Division, he scored 20.3 points per game (leading all Sonics players). Durant also led his team in total points scored (1,624), blocked shots (75), steals (78), free throws made (391), field goals made and attempted (587/1,366), minutes played (2,768), and games played and started (80).

Durant's efforts in his **inaugural** season earned him a spot on the all-rookie team and Rookie of the Year honors. This start to his NBA career was only the beginning of the many honors Durant would garner over the twelve years that he has played so far.

Durant was not only named to the All-Rookie team in his first season, but he was named Rookie of the Year as well.

KEVIN DURANT

POWER FORWARD

- Date of birth: September 29, 1988

- Height: 6 feet 9 inches (2.06 m)
  Weight: Approximately 240 pounds
  (109 kg)

- College: University of Texas (nickname:
  "Longhorns")

- Drafted in the first round in 2007
  (second pick overall) by the Seattle
  Supersonics (now Oklahoma City)

- Two-time NBA Champion (with Golden
  State Warriors), 2016–2018

- NBA Rookie of the Year, 2007–2008

- NBA Most Valuable Player, 2013–2014
  (as a member of the Oklahoma City
  Thunder)

- Five-time All-NBA first team, 2009–
  2014: 2017–2018)

- Two-time Olympic gold medalist (2012,
  2016)

- Most Valuable Player of the All-Star
  Game, 2011–2012

DURANT ON THE HARDWOOD

Durant has put up incredible statistics over the course of his NBA career. He has started every game that he has played in (803, through the 2018–2019 season). Durant has led the league in points per game in four of his twelve seasons (2010–2012, 2014), field goals made three times (2010, 2012, 2014), free throws made five times (210 – 2014), and points scored five times (2010–2014).

Durant has moved past players like the great Larry Bird and Clyde Drexler into the top thirty on the all-time points scored list. He has also moved into the top 75 all-time in several other offensive and defensive categories:

Durant has been a prolific scorer since his very first season in the NBA.

- Field goals made
- Field goals attempted
- Free throws made
- Free throws attempted
- Defensive rebounds
- Points per game

Here are Durant's year-by-year production statistics through the 2018–2019 NBA season:

Career Statistics

Season	G	FG	3P	FT	REB	AST	STL	BLK	PTS
2007–08	80	587	59	391	348	192	78	75	1,624
2008–09	74	661	97	452	482	205	96	53	1,871
2009–10	82	794	128	756	623	231	112	84	2,472
2010–11	78	711	145	594	533	214	88	76	2,161
2011–12	66	643	133	431	527	231	88	77	1,850
2012–13	81	731	139	679	640	374	116	105	2,280
2013–14	81	849	192	703	598	445	103	59	2,593
2014–15	27	238	64	146	178	110	24	25	686
2015–16	72	698	186	447	589	361	69	85	2,029
2016–17	62	551	117	336	513	300	66	99	1,555
2017–18	68	630	173	359	464	366	50	119	1,792
2018–19	78	721	137	448	497	457	58	84	2,027
TOTALS	849	7,814	1,570	5,742	5,992	3,486	948	941	22,940

Highlighted areas indicate statistics where he ranked first for the season in that category.

Durant Ds up on former teammate James Harden during the 2013 playoffs.

Durant's teams have made playoffs in nearly every season (except for the 2014–2015 season) since his rookie season of 2009-2010. Durant's playoff run has included seven Western Conference finals and four NBA Finals appearances. Of the four times he appeared in the NBA Finals, he has won two, with back-to-back championships (2017 and 2018 as a member of the Golden State Warriors). Here are Durant's playoffs statistics:

Playoff Statistics

Season	G	FG	3P	FT	REB	AST	STL	BLK	PTS
2009–10	6	43	10	54	46	14	3	8	150
2010–11	17	155	37	140	139	48	16	19	487
2011–12	20	198	41	133	148	74	29	24	570
2012–13	11	112	22	93	99	69	14	12	339
2013–14	19	194	43	132	170	75	19	25	563
2015–16	18	175	31	130	128	60	18	18	511
2016–17	*15*	*149*	*38*	*92*	*119*	*64*	*12*	*20*	*428*
2017–18	*21*	*212*	*47*	*137*	*163*	*99*	*15*	*25*	*608*
2018–19	*12*	*125*	*35*	*102*	*59*	*54*	*13*	*12*	*387*
TOTALS	139	1,363	304	1,013	1,071	557	139	163	4,047

Won NBA Championship

Durant has been named to the NBA All-Star Game as a member of the Western Conference team every season since the 2009–2010 season, a span of 10 consecutive seasons. He was named MVP of both the 2012 and 2019 games, where he scored 36 and 31 points respectively. For his 10 appearances Durant has averaged 25 points per game.

All-Star Game Statistics

Season	G	FG	3P	FT	TRB	AST	STL	BLK	PTS
2009–10	1	7	1	0	5	0	0	0	15
2010–11	1	11	4	8	3	2	2	2	34
2011–12	*1*	*14*	*3*	*5*	*7*	*3*	*3*	*0*	*36*
2012–13	1	13	3	1	6	1	2	0	30
2013–14	1	14	6	4	10	6	1	0	38
2014–15	1	1	1	0	3	1	1	0	3
2015–16	1	11	1	0	5	7	2	0	23
2016–17	1	9	2	1	10	10	2	0	21
2017–18	1	7	3	2	6	5	3	1	19
2018-19	1	10	6	5	7	2	1	2	31
TOTALS	**10**	**97**	**30**	**26**	**62**	**37**	**17**	**5**	**250**

Named All-Star Game MVP

Durant and his Golden State teammates ride in the victory parade for his first NBA championship in 2017.

50-40-90 CLUB MEMBER

One honor that Durant has earned is membership in the NBA's exclusive 50-40-90 club. The club is an achievement for those players who in a season have shot 50 percent or above (field goal percentage), 40 percent or above in three-point shots made (three-point percentage), and 90 percent or higher in free throws made (free throw percentage). He is one of only seven players in the history of the league who has achieved club status, which includes teammate Stephen Curry.

Although he is not known as a three-point shooter, everything seemed to fall in place for Durant during his 2012–2013 season with the Oklahoma City Thunder. He earned membership in the 50-40-90 club with 51 percent field-goal shooting, 41.6 percent three-point shooting, and 90.5 percent free throw shooting.

DURANT VS. THE BEST
[MAGIC, BIRD, ERVING, AND OTHERS]

Durant's career compares favorably to several players who have been in the NBA over the years. At 6 feet 9 inches (2.06 m) tall, he has the ability to play all three positions on the floor: center, forward, and guard. This means that for comparison's sake, it is best compare his career numbers against the best players in all positions, not just the forward position that he plays.

Durant became the second-youngest player to score 20,000 career points. A per-season average of 1,911 should put him close to the top in the scoring category, should he play another ten years (minimum). This seems to be possible for him to achieve, considering he entered the league after one year of college at the young age of nineteen years old.

Here is how his numbers compare to those of some of the best position players in NBA history:

Player	Years	G	GS	FG	FG%	FT	FT%	TRB	PTS
Karl Malone[†]	19	1,476	1,471	13,528	51.6%	9,787	74.2%	14,968	36,928
Dirk Nowitzki	21	1,522	1,460	11,169	47.1%	7,240	87.9%	11,489	31,560
Julius Erving[†]	16	1,243	442	11,818	50.6%	6,256	77.7%	10,525	30,026
Tim Duncan	19	1,392	1,389	10,285	50.6%	5,896	69.6%	15,091	26,496
Kevin Garnett	21	1,462	1,425	10,505	49.7%	4,887	78.9%	14,662	26,071
Charles Barkley[†]	16	1,073	1,012	8,435	54.1%	6,349	73.5%	12,546	23,757
Adrian Dantley	15	955	546	8,169	54.0%	6,832	81.8%	5,455	23,177

Player	Years	G	GS	FG	FG%	FT	FT%	TRB	PTS
Kevin Durant	12	849	849	7,814	49.3%	5,742	88.3%	5,992	22,940
Larry Bird[†]	13	897	870	8,591	49.6%	3,960	88.6%	8,974	21,791
Bob Pettit	11	792	0	7,349	43.6%	6,182	76.1%	12,849	20,880
Dolph Schayes[†]	15	996	0	5,863	38.0%	6,712	84.9%	11,256	18,438

[†]Member of the Hall of Fame

DURANT VS. HIS HERO, VINCE CARTER

Growing up, Durant was a big fan of the NBA. His favorite team was the Toronto Raptors and its star, Vince Carter. Known as "Vinsanity," Carter has played 21 seasons in the NBA, including the 2018–2019 season as a member of the Atlanta Hawks. His longtime **tenure** with the Toronto Raptors has earned him the nickname "Air Canada," and he has done a lot to increase fan interest in the game in the country of Canada.

Durant's numbers stack up well against those of Carter, and he will outpace his idol in no time:

Player	Years	G	GS	FG	FG%	FT	FT%	TRB	PTS
Vince Carter	21	1,432	982	9,059	43.7%	4,798	79.9%	6,353	25,061
Kevin Durant	12	849	849	7,814	49.3%	5,742	88.3%	5,992	22,940

Durant compares more than favorably to new stars, old stars, and even the player he looked up to as a kid watching basketball on TV. Maybe someday a younger version of himself watching the way he makes shots and wins games will pass the phenomenal numbers he has been able to put up in his NBA career.

Durant grew up idolizing long time NBA veteran Vince Carter, here about to dunk on his former team, Toronto. Carter has played 21 NBA seasons. He entered the league when Durant was ten years old.

TEXT-DEPENDENT QUESTIONS

1. Which NBA player did Durant look up to as a kid? What team was this player a member of in the 2018–2019 NBA season?

2. When did Durant first appear in the NBA playoffs? What team did he play for in his first playoff series?

3. What year did he first appear in an NBA All-Star Game? How many NBA All-Star Games has he participated in as a player?

 # RESEARCH PROJECT

Reaching 20,000 points in an NBA career is a remarkable accomplishment for any player. Doing this as fast as Durant has (second-fastest in league history) seems to indicate that he is on track to leave the game as one of its best scorers. Looking at the top ten players on the career points scored list, determine the age at which each reached that milestone (year and month; e.g., Durant was age twenty-nine years, three months when he scored 20,000 points). Then rank each by their age and add those ages and divide by ten to determine what the average age is for the top ten scorers in NBA history.

WORDS TO UNDERSTAND

conducive: Tending to produce; contributive; helpful

manifested: Made evident or certain by showing or displaying

respectively: In precisely the order given; sequentially

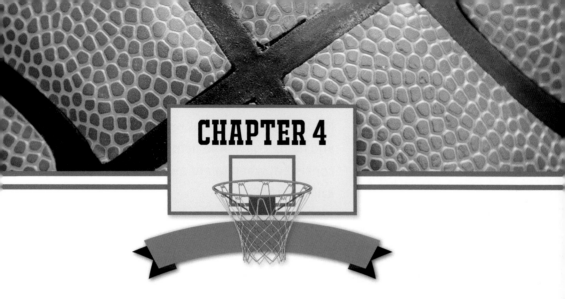

CHAPTER 4

WORDS COUNT

When the time comes to address the media before or after a game, players either retreat to the comfort of traditional phrases that avoid controversy (Cliché City), or they speak their mind with refreshing candor (Quote Machine).

Here are ten quotes, compiled in part from the website BrainyQuotes.com and others, with some insight as to the context of what Durant is talking about or referencing:

Durant has excelled at every level of the game as a player. This was due in part to his abnormal growth as an adolescent. Being six feet (1.83 m) tall as a thirteen-year-old pretty much suggests that you should give basketball a try. Along with his height, Durant developed shooting and other talents that helped him earn

"Hard work beats talent when talent fails to work hard."

McDonald's All-American status while in high school in 2006 and become a player of the year and most valuable player in college and the pros, respectively. Even though he possesses a tremendous amount of skill and talent, Durant knows that these will only carry him so far, especially

Durant was the last draft pick of the Seattle SuperSonics. The team moved to Oklahoma City after his rookie season in 2008.

in a league where he is one of many players possessing similar abilities. It is not an original idea by any means, but working hard, practicing, and being coachable helps Durant remain consistent when talent alone is not enough. **Rating: Cliché City**

> ## "I'm just trying to grow. That's one thing I told myself is, don't worry about who people say is the best player."

Durant played on two NBA teams in his first twelve NBA seasons: the Seattle Supersonics/Oklahoma City Thunder and Golden State Warriors. He has been a standout player on both of these squads, despite playing alongside some of the game's best current players like James Harden, Russell Westbrook, and Stephen Curry. Durant has been compared favorably to some of the greatest players in NBA history like Charles Barkley, Larry Bird, Bob Pettit, and Julius Erving. Despite the comparisons to past performers and the success that he has experienced, Durant continues to grow and work hard, learning what he can to become even better as a player and as a teammate. Others may determine who the best players are in the league; he would rather let his play speak for itself. **Rating: Quote Machine**

> ## "It's all about doing it for somebody I love. It's not what's the better number and what looks better on me. It's all about him."

Durant's early mentor and AAU coach Charles "Big Chucky" Craig died as a result of a senseless act of violence at the age of thirty-five in 2005. The loss of an adult who was so important to his development not only as a basketball player but also as a person is honored each time he puts on a basketball uniform. Durant, while playing at the University of Texas and for his first 12 NBA seasons wore number "35" as a silent tribute to the

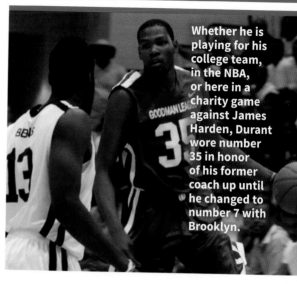

Whether he is playing for his college team, in the NBA, or here in a charity game against James Harden, Durant wore number 35 in honor of his former coach up until he changed to number 7 with Brooklyn.

memory of a coach who was conducive to Durant becoming an NBA star and a successful person in life. **Rating: Quote Machine**

"**Every memory I had growing up was involving a basketball. I didn't go to the prom and stuff like that. It was always basketball for me.**"

Basketball is more than a job or career for Durant. It has been everything for him, and that passion is the reason he has risen to the heights he has as one of the league's leading superstars. Durant indicates with this quote that all of his memories from the beginning involved a basketball in one way or another. He grew up in the Washington, DC, area with dreams of playing in the NBA for his favorite team, the Toronto Raptors, and with his personal hero at the time, Vince Carter. As he played for AAU and prep teams in his area, he developed the abilities that took him to the University of Texas and then the NBA.
Rating: Quote Machine

"My mom just wants to make sure that my heart is always in whatever I do and I'm in things for the right reasons."

Durant's mother, Wanda Durant, is an important part of his life. For a long time she was the only parent that he knew. She made the sacrifices that parents make to ensure the success of their children. This was doubly important to her as she was also a single parent raising four children and working full-time. She has spoken of her own disappointments and challenges but always made sure to support (and push) her son in making good choices and dedicating himself to giving 100 percent of his effort. **Rating: Quote Machine**

WANDA DURANT, THE REAL MVP

Durant grew up outside of Washington, DC, in a town called Suitland, Maryland. His parents split up just about the time he was one year old, and he was raised mostly by his mother, Wanda Durant. Although his father would again become a part of his life when he turned thirteen, most of his development into adulthood came under the direction of his mother. Durant learned from her the lessons of hard work and not giving up on your dreams. Once, while working for the federal government, she was turned down for a promotion. She turned the disappointment into motivation to work harder instead of quitting. This is something she instilled in all of her children; her commitment to that lesson has **manifested** itself not only in Durant becoming a star in the NBA but in her realizing a dream and becoming a motivational speaker and philanthropist in her own right.

Durant pays tribute to the most important person in his life, his mother, Wanda Durant, who is known affectionately by everyone as Mama Durant, the Real MVP.

"People always think women meet us in the hotel lobby, but it's the opposite. The majority of the time, you go out to eat with your teammates, then rest for the next day's game. It's not a vacation—most guys view the road as a business trip." Durant challenges the myth that being an NBA superstar means a life of constant parties and women chasing players through hotel lobbies. That type of life is not one that he has experienced in his career. What Durant describes is a life that is no different than any other person who goes off to work every day. The NBA may be a more glamorous job than most people have, but it does involve work. For most players, especially those

Durant says life on the road with the Warriors is all work and no play.

with Durant's skill level, the job of being a professional basketball player revolves around going to practice, meeting with coaches, receiving physical therapy for their sore and aching bodies, and getting rest—this, while also signing autographs for fans, attempting to eat in peace, and finding a moment to be alone with their own thoughts. **Rating: Quote Machine**

> **"I'm busy working on every aspect of my game—defense, shooting, rebounding—but I really want to become a better overall team player. Help my teammates become better players out on the court in order to win more ball games."**

Durant has the statistics to back up the individual parts of his game. He can score, rebound, dish out assists, and block shots. This seems to be something that comes naturally to a person who is six feet nine inches (2.06 m) tall and has the fingertip-to-fingertip wingspan of seven feet five inches (2.26 m). Having good individual stats is important for the Warriors and was a difference-maker in the 2016–2017 season when the Warriors won the NBA Championship. Durant wants to continue to grow and develop as a player and not only turn in great individual stats but also do more to help his teammates be better as a team and not just individuals. Hopefully he will also want to work on turning in great individual quotes rather than clichés like this one. **Rating: Cliché City.**

> **"You know, I think more people should watch women's basketball. It'd do so much for the game."**

The Women's National Basketball Association (WNBA) was formed, in part by the NBA, in 1997, as a way for the country's (and the world's) best female players to perform at the professional level. It has not been as popular as its male counterpart (the NBA), but through the financial support of the NBA it has remained afloat. Although the NBA remains committed to the success of the WNBA as an expression of women's professional sports, Durant suggests that more can be done to support the WNBA if more NBA fans just watch.
Rating: Quote Machine

Very few players in the history of the NBA have experienced the level of success that Durant has in such a short period of time. He is a two-time NBA champion. He has received all-rookie and Rookie of the Year honors, been named a league MVP, an all-star game MVP, and an NBA Finals MVP. Durant has played on nine all-star teams and been named to eight all-NBA squads. Those accomplishments, along with Olympic gold medals for representing the U.S. Men's National Basketball Team at the London Summer Olympics in 2012 and Rio de Janeiro Summer Olympics in 2016, are more than any one player would ever expect to experience in a lifetime, let alone a short twelve-year career. **Rating: Quote Machine**

> **"Everything has been such a whirlwind ever since I stepped foot in the league and everything has been like a dream, so I'm just blessed to be in this position."**

Durant is a two-time gold medalist for representing his country at the Summer Olympic Games.

Durant began making appearances in all-star games and being named to all-NBA teams in 2009. The consistency in this type of recognition means that of the 450 players in the league, he has been among the ten best nearly every year since 2009. Durant doesn't measure himself by the success he has experienced among those he plays with but rather by the standard set by those players who were in the league before him. He is often considered one of the three best players in the NBA along with teammate Stephen Curry and LeBron James of the Los Angeles Lakers. He feels that he is now coming to a point where his star will rise even more as he is in the prime years of his career.

"I've got a long way to go to being the ultimate best, but I think my time is now. And I'm starting to enter my prime."

Rating: Quote Machine

TEXT-DEPENDENT QUESTIONS

1. What number does Durant wear on his NBA jersey? When did he first start wearing the number? In whose honor does he wear the number?

2. How tall was Durant (in feet and meters) when he turned thirteen years old? How tall is he today?

3. Which Olympic Games (year and place) did Durant participate in as a member of the U.S. Men's National Basketball Team?

 # RESEARCH PROJECT

Durant, while in middle school, grew to nearly six feet (1.83 m) tall. That is unusually tall for a middle schooler, but a further growth spurt had him shoot up to nearly six feet eight inches (2.03 m) by his sophomore year in high school (about two years later). That size put him in position to become a great NBA player. As unusual as it is for most of us to imagine growing so tall so quickly, it is not as unusual for prospective NBA players. There are several players, a few, in fact, that currently play in the NBA, who experienced rapid growth spurts while in high school. Name five players who experienced a growth spurt of at least five inches or more in one year (Hint: Durant played with one of them). Identify the team they play (or played) for, how tall they were at the start of their growth spurt, and their current height.

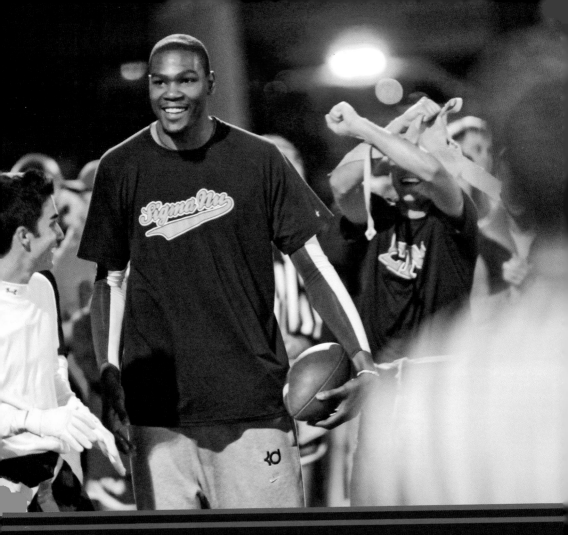

 ## WORDS TO UNDERSTAND

initiative: A plan or program that is intended to solve a problem

gangly: Tall and thin, and moving with a loose-jointed awkwardness; lanky

signature: Something (such as a tune, style, or logo) that serves to set apart or identify

CHAPTER 5

OFF THE COURT

DURANT AT HOME

Durant signed a two-year contract extension in 2018 with the Golden State Warriors worth $61.5 million. Having that amount of money available to you can certainly help finance the purchase of a 5,136 square-foot (1,565.45 square-meter) multilevel home in Malibu, California. The home was purchased for the price of $12.05 million. It has perfect views of the Pacific Ocean off its not one, not two, not three, but four outdoor decks (including one on the rooftop).

The home is a good place for Durant to establish roots in the community and is a far cry from the many apartments he shared with his mother, Wanda, and his siblings in Suitland. He currently lives alone, as he is not married nor does he have children.

THE IMPORTANCE OF EDUCATION

After one year at the University of Texas, Durant left school to pursue his childhood dream of playing in the NBA. Although he left school early and has made no indication about his own future as it relates to obtaining a degree, he nonetheless supports and advocates on behalf of youth to obtain an education. He believes in providing education opportunities, especially considering his own background, growing up in a single-parent household in a low-income area of the Washington, DC, area.

He recently partnered with College Track, an Oakland, CA-based 501(c)3 organization, whose mission is "to empower students from underserved communities to graduate from college. By helping students maximize the value of their college degree—minimize student loan debt, secure internships, and limit the need to work while in college—we prepare today's youth to succeed in the 21st-century economy."

Durant's partnership resulted in a pledge to provide $10 million in funds to help students in Prince George's County, Maryland (where Suitland is located), go to college. The $10 million, paid over ten years, will be used to establish The Durant Center Educational and Leadership Facility in his hometown of Suitland, Maryland.

Durant and his mother, Wanda Durant, pose for a photo with Maryland Lieutenant Governor Boyd Rutherford at Kevin Durant Day in his hometown of Seat Pleasant.

Durant is the unofficial advisor to the CEO of Alaska Airlines, the company he has partnered with to create education initiatives in the Bay area.

Durant has also partnered with Alaska Airlines, accepting the unofficial title of "Advisor to the CEO," in 2017. The exclusive arrangement with Alaska Airlines is in support of creating and supporting education initiatives in the Oakland–San Francisco Bay Area. As an advisor, Durant's role is to represent the airline at community events and activities that promote educational opportunities for youth. The partnership has also helped him receive from Alaska Airlines donations to his charitable foundation to help fund his "BUILD IT AND THEY WILL BALL" project.

THE CHARITY OF DURANT
KEVIN DURANT CHARITY FOUNDATION

The mission of the Kevin Durant Charity Foundation is "to enrich the lives of at-risk youths from ages six to eighteen through educational, athletic and social program support." The charity is based in Miami, Florida, with Durant serving as its principal officer. One of the key programs of foundation is to build basketball courts in low-income areas. This initiative, the BUILD IT AND THEY WILL BALL Courts Renovation Initiative, provides both athletic and educational facilities to enrich the lives of youth.

To date, the program has been active in building courts in the following cities in the United States and around the world:

- Oklahoma City, Oklahoma (two courts built in 2015)
- Berlin, Germany (built in 2015)

- Guangzhou, China (built in 2016)
- Austin, Texas (built in 2016)
- Seattle, Washington (built in 2016)
- Seat Pleasant, Maryland (two courts built in May 2017)
- Oakland, California (two courts built in May 2017)
- New York, New York (built in July 2017)
- New Delhi, India (two courts built in August 2017)
- Redwood City, California (built in September 2017)
- Taipei, Taiwan (built in July 2018)
- Washington, DC (two courts built in October 2018)
- San Francisco, California (two courts built in October 2018)

MARKETING DURANT

"THIRTY5"

The number "35" is what Durant wore until he went to Brooklyn. It is also the name of his investment and media companies, "Thirty5 Ventures" and "Thirty5 Media." They were formed by Durant in partnership with Rich Kleinman as cofounder. Kleinman is an NBA agent for Roc Nation Sports, the sports agency created by rap-mogul Shawn "Jay-Z" Carter and live event company Live Nation. Kleinman is also Durant's agent.

The number Durant wore growing up and for his first 12 NBA seasons is also the name of his investment and media companies.

His media company, Thirty5 Media, is involved in bringing to life stories from the community about the impact certain people have had on the lives of others. One of the projects that Thirty5 Media is engaged in is a documentary (in collaboration with Fox Sports) called *Q Ball*. The documentary focuses on the lives of men incarcerated in famed San Quentin Prison and how they use basketball as an outlet to cope with their situation. He has also partnered with Apple to produce a youth-themed series called *Swagger*.

Thirty5 Ventures is his investment company. He uses it as a way to fund promising start-ups and give hope to beginning entrepreneurs. Some of the ventures in which he has invested include the following:

- Acorns, a microinvesting app
- Coinbase, a digital currency exchange
- Lime, a national dockless rideshare program
- Postmates, online delivery service
- Robinhood, a self-directed investing app

MARKETING

Durant sports a t-shirt by Nike, one of the many companies he endorses.

According to *Forbes* magazine, Durant makes more than $30 million in off-court income. Much of those earnings come from endorsements of various products, such as Panini, Beats Electronics, Alaska Air Group, and Nike. His partnership with Nike has produced three different shoes (offered in children and adult sizes): the KD Zooms, KD 10s, and KD 11s.

KEEPING HIS SHOES ON

There is research (seriously!) that found that between the 2015 and 2017 seasons, Durant has lost a shoe once every eight games. That is an incredible statistic, even for someone who plays as much as he does. Fans curious as to why his shoes come loose so often during games posed the question to him, to which he responded, "I don't really tie 'em up that tight. I made my shoe (referencing his **signature** Nike KD 10 shoe) to fit me like a sock almost and be as light as I can."

Losing his shoe as much as he does doesn't affect Durant's overall ability to shoot and defend, but it takes him out of the play about once every eight games.

SALARY

Durant exercised his option to turn down a contract offer for the 2017–2018 season that would have paid him $27.7 million in salary. This was expected, as given his success and value to the Warriors, he could reasonably expect to receive an offer for the maximum possible of $38 million in salary for the season. However, Durant took a deal for less money and signed a two-year, $61.5 million contract on July 7, 2018. Not taking a max deal means Durant gave the Warriors some flexibility under the salary cap to keep key players and sign other good ones as needed. For example, before the 2018–2019 season, the Warriors were able to sign four-time All-Star DeMarcus Cousins.

The extension included $30 million for the 2018–2019 season and $31.5 million for the 2019–2020 season. The Warriors had hoped that this new deal would keep Durant in Oakland through the 2019-2020 season. However, the 2019-2020 portion of the contract included a player option for Durant, and he chose not to stay with Golden State. He announced that he would sign with the Brooklyn Nets instead. The Warriors and Nets ultimately worked out a sign and trade deal that saw Durant go east in exchange for D'Angelo Russell.

Here is a look at his year-by-year earnings, starting with his rookie contract with the Seattle Supersonics from the 2007–2008 season:

Season	Team	Salary
2007–08	Seattle SuperSonics	$ 4,171,200
2008–09	Oklahoma City Thunder	$ 4,484,040
2009–10	Oklahoma City Thunder	$ 4,796,880
2010–11	Oklahoma City Thunder	$ 6,053,663
2011–12	Oklahoma City Thunder	$ 15,506,632
2012–13	Oklahoma City Thunder	$ 16,669,630
2013–14	Oklahoma City Thunder	$ 17,832,627
2014–15	Oklahoma City Thunder	$ 18,995,624

Season	Team	Salary
2015–16	Oklahoma City Thunder	$ 20,158,622
2016–17	Golden State Warriors	$ 26,540,100
2017–18	Golden State Warriors	$ 25,000,000
		$ 160,209,018
2018–19	Golden State Warriors	$ 30,000,000
2019–20	Brooklyn Nets	$ 38,199,000
2020-21	Brooklyn Nets	$ 40,108,950
2021-22	Brooklyn Nets	$ 42,018,900
2022-23	Brooklyn Nets	$ 43,928,850
		$ 164,255,700
	TOTAL	$ 324,464,718

Durant has put himself in position to win several more NBA championships before he takes off his basketball shoes for good. He also may be the player everyone looks up to as the league's all-time scoring leader, based on the number of points he has already scored and the number of years he still has left to play. A lot of good things have happened for a once shy, **gangly** boy from Suitland, Maryland. He has taken advantage of his talents and opportunities to become one of the game's true greats!

Golden State was able to sign All-Star free agent DeMarcus Cousins in 2018 in part due to the reduced salary Durant agreed to on his 2018 contract.

TEXT-DEPENDENT QUESTIONS

1. What is the value of Durant's two-year contract extension signed with the Golden State Warriors in 2018?

2. What is the name of his agent? What agency represents Durant? What famous entertainment figure owns the agency that represents him?

3. How much has he pledged to give to students in Prince George's County, Maryland, to assist with college tuition?

 # RESEARCH PROJECT

Durant earns just about as much off-the-court income annually as he is paid for his performance on the court (currently). The $30 million he earns for the various outside endorsements he makes is more than enough for him to leave the game and retire comfortably for the rest of his life (which at age thirty-one may be a long time from now). Find five other NBA stars who earn more from their outside income than what they are paid for playing. Determine the amount they make annually, the source of this income (that is, from endorsements, acting, investing, etc.), and rank them in order of total income earned per year and the amount earned away from basketball.

assist: a pass that directly leads to a teammate making a basket.

blocked shot: when a defensive player stops a shot at the basket by hitting the ball away.

center: a player whose main job is to score near the basket and win offensive and defensive rebounds. Centers are usually the tallest players on the court, and the best are able to move with speed and agility.

double-dribble: when a player dribbles the ball with two hands or stops dribbling and starts again. The opposing team gets the ball.

field goal: a successful shot worth two points—three points if shot from behind the three-point line.

foul: called by the officials for breaking a rule: reaching in, blocking, charging, and over the back, for example. If a player commits six fouls during the game, he fouls out and must leave play. If an offensive player is fouled while shooting, he usually gets two foul shots (one shot if the player's basket counted or three if he was fouled beyond the three-point line).

foul shot: a "free throw," an uncontested shot taken from the foul line (15 feet [4.6 m]) from the basket.

goaltending: when a defensive player touches the ball after it has reached its highest point on the way to the basket. The team on offense gets the points they would have received from the basket. Goaltending is also called on any player, on offense or defense, who slaps the backboard or touches the ball directly above the basket.

jump ball: when an official puts the ball into play by tossing it in the air. Two opposing players try to tip it to their own teammate.

man-to-man defense: when each defensive player guards a single offensive player.

officials: those who monitor the action and call fouls. In the NBA there are three for each game.

point guard: the player who handles the ball most on offense. He brings the ball up the court and tries to create scoring opportunities through passing. Good point guards are quick, good passers, and can see the court well.

power forward: a player whose main jobs are to score from close to the basket and win offensive and defensive rebounds. Good power forwards are tall and strong.

rebound: when a player gains possession of the ball after a missed shot.

roster: the players on a team. NBA teams have twelve-player rosters.

shooting guard: a player whose main job is to score using jump shots and drives to the basket. Good shooting guards are usually taller than point guards but still quick.

shot clock: a twenty-four-second clock that starts counting down when a team gets the ball. The clock restarts whenever the ball changes possession. If the offense does not shoot the ball in time, it turns the ball over to the other team.

small forward: a player whose main job is to score from inside or outside. Good small forwards are taller than point or shooting guards and have speed and agility.

steal: when a defender takes the ball from an opposing player.

technical foul: called by the official for misconduct or a procedural violation. The team that does not commit the foul gets possession of the ball and a free throw.

three-point play: a two-point field goal combined with a successful free throw. This happens when an offensive player makes a basket but is fouled in the process.

three-point shot: a field goal made from behind the three-point line.

traveling: when a player moves, taking three steps or more, without dribbling, also called "walking." The opposing team gets the ball.

turnover: when the offensive team loses the ball: passing the ball out of bounds, traveling, or double-dribbling, for example.

zone defense: when each defensive player guards within a specific area of the court. Common zones include 2-1-2, 1-3-1, or 2-3. Zone defense has only recently been allowed in the NBA.

FURTHER READING

James, Steve. *Kevin Durant: Rise Above and Shoot, the Kevin Durant Story*. North Charleston, SC: CreateSpace Independent Publishing Platform, 2017.

Peyton, Steve. *Kevin Durant: The Inspirational Story of a Scoring Superstar*. North Charleston, SC: CreateSpace Independent Publishing Platform, 2016.

Thompson, Marcus. *KD: Kevin Durant's Relentless Pursuit to Be the Greatest*. New York: Atria Books, 2019.

Whiting, Jim. *The NBA: A History of Hoops—Golden State Warriors*. Mankato, MN: Creative Education, 2017.

INTERNET RESOURCES

https://www.basketball-reference.com/players/d/duranke01.html
The basketball-specific resource provided by Sports Reference, LLC for current and historical statistics of Kevin Durant.

http://bleacherreport.com/nba
The official website for Bleacher Report Sport's NBA reports on each of the thirty teams.

https://www.cbssports.com/nba/teams/GS/golden-state-warriors/
The web page for the Golden State Warriors provided by CBSSports.com, providing latest news and information, player profiles, scheduling, and standings.

https://www.eastbaytimes.com/sports/golden-state-warriors/
The web page of the *East Bay Times* (Oakland) newspaper for the Golden State Warriors basketball team.

www.espn.com/nba/team/_/name/gs/golden-state-warriors
The official website of ESPN sports network for the Golden State Warriors.

http://www.nba.com/#/
The official website of the National Basketball Association.

https://www.nba.com/warriors/
The official NBA website for the Golden State Warriors basketball team, including history, player information, statistics, and news.

https://sports.yahoo.com/nba/
The official website of Yahoo! Sports NBA coverage, providing news, statistics, and important information about the association and its thirty teams.

INDEX

INDEX

INDEX

EDUCATIONAL VIDEO LINKS

Pg. 12: http://x-qr.net/1KdY

Pg. 18: http://x-qr.net/1MA2

Pg. 13: http://x-qr.net/1KJF

Pg. 19: http://x-qr.net/1K06

Pg. 14: http://x-qr.net/1KVy

Pg. 29: http://x-qr.net/1KZF

Pg. 15: http://x-qr.net/1K9s

Pg. 49: http://x-qr.net/1JGD

Pg. 16: http://x-qr.net/1JA2

Pg. 59: http://x-qr.net/1M5D

Pg. 17: http://x-qr.net/1LPH

Pg. 70: http://x-qr.net/1Lvb

PHOTO CREDITS

AUTHOR BIOGRAPHY

Donald Parker is an avid sports fan, author, and father. He enjoys watching and participating in many types of sports, including football, basketball, baseball, and golf. He enjoyed a brief career as a punter and defensive back at NCAA Division III Carroll College (now University) in Waukesha, Wisconsin, and spends much of his time now watching and writing about the sports he loves.